QUICK & EASY
SOUPS

70 imaginative recipes
for the busy cook

Myra Street

Howell Press

© 1994 Salamander Books Ltd.

HOWELL PRESS
Published in the United States 1994 by
Howell Press, Inc., 1147 River Road,
Suite 2, Charlottesville, VA 22901
Telephone 804-977-4006

ISBN: 0-943231-67-1

Managing Editor Samantha Gray
Art Director Jane Forster
Photographer Sue Jorgensen
Home Economists Myra Street and Rowena Coventry
Typeset by Bookworm Typesetting, Manchester
Colour Separation by Scantrans Pte. Ltd., Singapore
Jacket Border by Susan Williams (Home Economist)
Edward Allwright (Photographer)
Acorn Studios plc, London
(Computer Graphics)

Printed and bound by Proost International Book Production

Contents

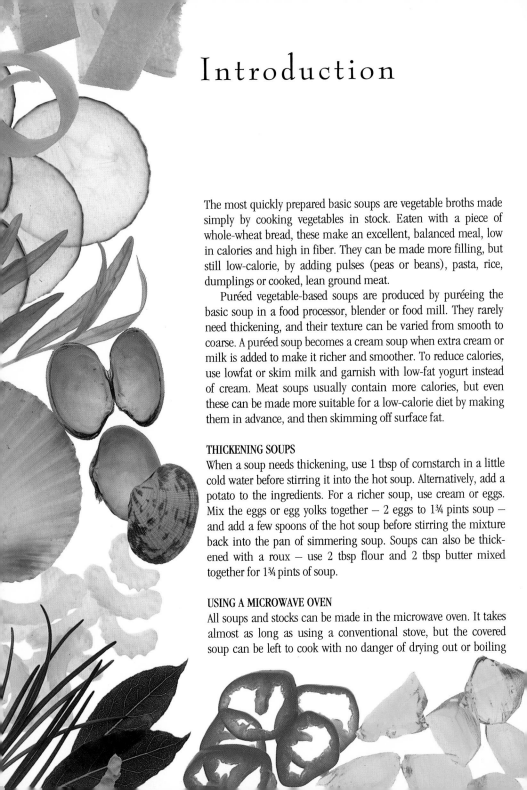

Introduction

The most quickly prepared basic soups are vegetable broths made simply by cooking vegetables in stock. Eaten with a piece of whole-wheat bread, these make an excellent, balanced meal, low in calories and high in fiber. They can be made more filling, but still low-calorie, by adding pulses (peas or beans), pasta, rice, dumplings or cooked, lean ground meat.

Puréed vegetable-based soups are produced by puréeing the basic soup in a food processor, blender or food mill. They rarely need thickening, and their texture can be varied from smooth to coarse. A puréed soup becomes a cream soup when extra cream or milk is added to make it richer and smoother. To reduce calories, use lowfat or skim milk and garnish with low-fat yogurt instead of cream. Meat soups usually contain more calories, but even these can be made more suitable for a low-calorie diet by making them in advance, and then skimming off surface fat.

THICKENING SOUPS

When a soup needs thickening, use 1 tbsp of cornstarch in a little cold water before stirring it into the hot soup. Alternatively, add a potato to the ingredients. For a richer soup, use cream or eggs. Mix the eggs or egg yolks together — 2 eggs to 1¾ pints soup — and add a few spoons of the hot soup before stirring the mixture back into the pan of simmering soup. Soups can also be thickened with a roux — use 2 tbsp flour and 2 tbsp butter mixed together for 1¾ pints of soup.

USING A MICROWAVE OVEN

All soups and stocks can be made in the microwave oven. It takes almost as long as using a conventional stove, but the covered soup can be left to cook with no danger of drying out or boiling over. Cook any finely chopped root vegetables first in the stock until tender, then add green vegetables and herbs for the required cooking time.

To make 1¾ pints of stock, use about 2 pounds chopped bones, 1¾ pints water, 1 carrot, 1 onion and a bouquet garni if liked. Cover with microwave-safe plastic wrap and cook on High (100%) for 30 minutes.

STORING SOUPS

With the exception of fish soups, which should be eaten soon after cooking, soups can be stored in the refrigerator for several days. But take care when reheating them to bring them to a rolling boil and boil for several minutes.

Most soups freeze extremely well, so save time by making a larger quantity than you need. Pour the cooled soup into a plastic bag lining a square box. Freeze, then remove the bag from the box and seal with a twist tie, leaving ½ inch head space. Label and stack soup packages one on top of the other in the freezer.

When a soup is to be frozen, leave out the major seasoning until reheating. It is also better to add pasta, rice and shellfish to thawed soup during reheating. Do not freeze soups containing eggs and cream.

STOCKS FOR SOUP

Keep stock for only 2 days in the refrigerator, then boil and cool before storing again. Stock containing root vegetables will keep for only a few days and is best frozen if you don't use it immediately.

BROWN STOCK

Use brown stock for dark soups.

Ingredients: Beef or veal bones; ¼ cup butter or 4 tbsp oil; vegetables and herbs as for white stock (page 8).

Heat the butter or oil in a roasting pan in the oven at 400°F. Add the bones and allow to brown for 40 minutes.

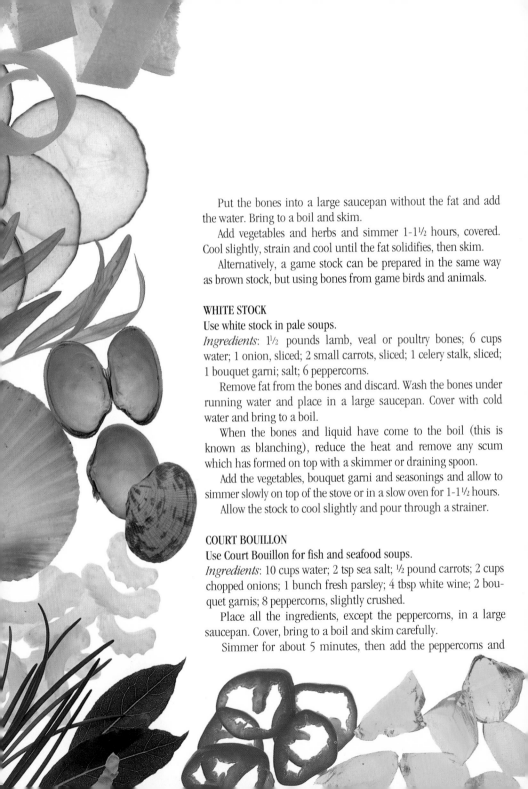

Put the bones into a large saucepan without the fat and add the water. Bring to a boil and skim.

Add vegetables and herbs and simmer 1-1½ hours, covered. Cool slightly, strain and cool until the fat solidifies, then skim.

Alternatively, a game stock can be prepared in the same way as brown stock, but using bones from game birds and animals.

WHITE STOCK
Use white stock in pale soups.

Ingredients: 1½ pounds lamb, veal or poultry bones; 6 cups water; 1 onion, sliced; 2 small carrots, sliced; 1 celery stalk, sliced; 1 bouquet garni; salt; 6 peppercorns.

Remove fat from the bones and discard. Wash the bones under running water and place in a large saucepan. Cover with cold water and bring to a boil.

When the bones and liquid have come to the boil (this is known as blanching), reduce the heat and remove any scum which has formed on top with a skimmer or draining spoon.

Add the vegetables, bouquet garni and seasonings and allow to simmer slowly on top of the stove or in a slow oven for 1-1½ hours.

Allow the stock to cool slightly and pour through a strainer.

COURT BOUILLON
Use Court Bouillon for fish and seafood soups.

Ingredients: 10 cups water; 2 tsp sea salt; ½ pound carrots; 2 cups chopped onions; 1 bunch fresh parsley; 4 tbsp white wine; 2 bouquet garnis; 8 peppercorns, slightly crushed.

Place all the ingredients, except the peppercorns, in a large saucepan. Cover, bring to a boil and skim carefully.

Simmer for about 5 minutes, then add the peppercorns and

continue cooking for about 20 minutes. Allow to cool, then strain through a fine strainer.

To use, simmer the fish gently in the liquid and remove when cooked, then strain the liquid.

BEET STOCK

Ingredients: 1 large beet, preferably uncooked; boiling stock or water; 3 tbsp wine vinegar.

Wash the earth from the beet and grate it directly into the pan to prevent any juice being lost.

Pour in enough boiling stock or water to cover the beet. Add the vinegar and bring slowly to a boil.

Remove from the heat and allow to stand for 30 minutes.

Strain into beet soup just before serving. Don't boil after you have added it or the color will spoil.

VEGETABLE STOCK

Ingredients: 1 tbsp olive oil; 4 potatoes, cut into even-sized pieces; 1 large onion, sliced; 2 carrots, chopped; 2 celery stalks, chopped; 1 bay leaf; 1 bouquet garni; sprig of parsley or thyme; 6 cups water.

To make a light vegetable stock:

Heat the oil in a large saucepan, add all the chopped vegetables and cook over a low heat, stirring from time to time. Do not allow the vegetables to color.

Pour in the water, bring to a boil and allow to simmer for about 1½ hours, making sure the liquid does not evaporate.

Strain the stock and cool. Store in the refrigerator for up to 3 days. For longer storage, use the freezer.

To make a dark vegetable stock:

Heat 2 tbsp oil and fry the onion on a medium heat until golden. Add the remaining vegetables and allow to brown. Add miso or soy sauce to the water and simmer.

Beet Consommé

INGREDIENTS

Serves 6-8

2 quarts clarified beef
or chicken stock

2 large cooked beets,
peeled

1 tsp lemon juice

salt and pepper

⅔ cup sour cream

1 tbsp snipped chives

1   Pour the stock into a large pan.

2   Chop the beets into small dice and retain 3 tablespoons.

3   Add the remaining beets to the stock. Do not allow the mixture to boil, but just simmer gently.

4   Add the remainder of the beets and allow to simmer without bubbling for 5 minutes.

5   Strain into a warmed bowl, add the lemon juice and taste for seasoning.

6   Serve with the sour cream, whipped until slightly thick, with chives sprinkled on top.

COOK'S TIP
Cut some cooked beets into interesting shapes with small pastry cutters to add to the consommé before serving.

Cream Cheese Consommé

1   Dissolve the gelatin in a little hot consommé. Add to the remainder of the consommé.

2   Divide the consommé between six wine glasses. Chill in the refrigerator until set.

3   Mix the soft cheese and sour cream with the lemon juice, paprika and seasoning. Smooth on top of the jellied consommé.

4   Sprinkle with chives and serve with crisp triangles of toast.

COOK'S TIP
Chicken or beef consommé can be used for this appetizer (canned or homemade). The cheese mixture can also be made with low fat cream cheese mixed with curry powder and chopped herbs.

INGREDIENTS

Serves 6

1 envelope unflavored gelatin

2 ½ cups beet or other consommé (see page 10)

½ cups low fat cream cheese

½ cup sour cream

1 tbsp lemon juice

½ tsp paprika

salt and pepper

2 tsp snipped chives

Beef Consommé

INGREDIENTS

Makes 1 quart

½ pound shin of beef

2 celery stalks, finely
chopped

2 carrots, diced

2 leeks, green tops only,
chopped

2 tomatoes, chopped

2 egg whites and shells

6 cups beef stock,
strained and without fat
(see page 7)

salt and pepper

1-2 tbsp sherry (optional)

1　Remove all the fat from the beef and grind or put it through a food processor. Add all the vegetables and mix together thoroughly.

2　Beat the egg whites until just frothy. Add to the meat and vegetable mixture and stir gently to mix.

3　Heat the stock very slowly over a low heat just enough to make sure any jelly is melted.

4　Pour the stock onto the meat mixture and mix thoroughly. Return to the saucepan. Crush the egg shells in a bowl.

5　Whisk the mixture until frothy on a medium heat. Add the egg shells and allow the stock to come to a boil. Lower the heat and, with a ladle, make a hole in the solid layer to enable the consommé to bubble without breaking up the substance which is clarifying beneath.

6　Simmer very gently for 30 minutes to gain maximum flavor. The liquid will clarify and the filter will form a solid crust.

7　Place a piece of damp cheesecloth or a clean, non woven cloth in a strainer. Gently break up the filter and strain the consommé through the cloth. Allow to cool. Add the sherry just before serving.

Chicken Consommé

1 Remove all fat and skin from raw chicken. Chop the chicken meat finely or purée in a food processor.

2 Put the chicken in a bowl with all the vegetables and mix.

3 In another bowl, beat the egg whites until just frothy. Add to the meat and vegetable mixture, then stir gently to mix.

4 Heat the stock in a saucepan slowly over low heat to make sure any jelly is melted. Do not allow to boil.

5 Pour the stock onto the chicken mixture and stir well. Return to the saucepan.

6 Crush the egg shells in a plastic bag. Beat the chicken mixture over a medium heat until some froth appears.

7 Add the egg shells to the mixture in the pan and allow the liquid to come to a boil slowly.

8 Lower the heat and make a hole in the solid crust with a ladle to enable the mixture to bubble through. Simmer very gently for 30 minutes. A solid crust will form.

9 Strain the consommé through damp cheesecloth.

INGREDIENTS

Makes 1 quart

½ pound chicken giblets, washed

½ pound chicken, skinned

1 small onion, finely chopped
1 carrot, finely chopped
2 stalks celery, finely chopped
2 leeks, green tops only, chopped
2 tomatoes, chopped

2 egg whites and shells

6 cups strained fat-free chicken stock

salt and pepper

2 tbsp sherry

Carrot and Coriander Soup

INGREDIENTS

Serves 4

¼ cup butter

1 onion, sliced

1 pound carrots, sliced

4 celery stalks, sliced

1 tsp ground coriander

½ tsp ground cumin

4½ cups chicken or
vegetable stock

salt and pepper

2 tbsp chopped fresh
coriander

whole-wheat croutons

1   Heat the butter in a large saucepan. Add the onion, carrots and celery. Stir and allow the vegetables to absorb the butter.

2   Turn up the heat slightly and add the coriander and cumin. Stir briskly into the vegetables for 2 minutes.

3   Add the stock and stir until the ingredients are well mixed. Bring to a boil, cover and simmer for 25 minutes. Allow to cool.

4   Purée the soup in a food processor or blender, or pass through a food mill. Season and reheat gently, sprinkle with chopped coriander and serve with whole-wheat croutons.

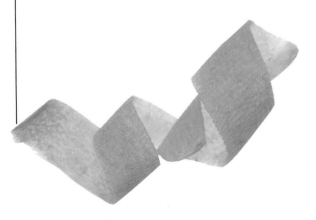

Tomato and Rice Soup

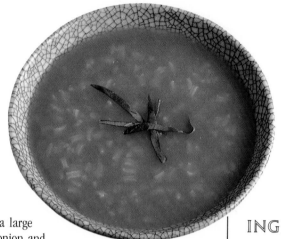

1   Heat butter in a large saucepan. Add the onion and allow to cook over a low heat for a few minutes until transparent. Stir from time to time.

2   Stir the celery into the onions. Cook for about 2 minutes, then add the carrots, tomatoes and juice, oregano, tomato paste, half the stock, bouquet garni, sugar and seasoning.

3   Bring to a boil slowly, cover and allow to simmer for about 20 minutes.

4   Remove the bouquet garni and bay leaf. Rub through a wide-meshed strainer or food mill, or purée in a food processor.

5   Add the remaining stock, a little salt if needed and the rice. Cook for about 10 minutes.

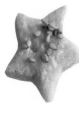

6   Serve in heated bowls sprinkled with chopped celery leaves.

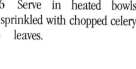

INGREDIENTS

Serves 4

2 tbsp butter

2 onions, chopped

2 celery stalks, chopped

2 carrots, diced

14½ oz can tomatoes

¼ tsp or 2 sprigs oregano

1 tbsp tomato paste

4½ cups chicken stock

1 bouquet garni

1 tsp sugar

¼ cup long-grain rice

1 tbsp chopped celery leaves

Tomato and Orange Soup

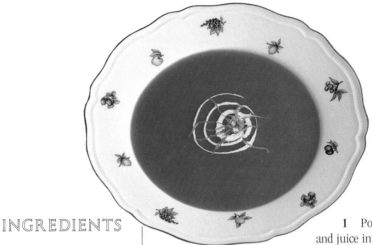

INGREDIENTS

Serves 6

4 x 14½ oz cans plum
tomatoes

1 onion, sliced
1 carrot, chopped

1 strip of lemon zest and
2 strips orange zest

1 bouquet garni
6 peppercorns
salt
4½ cups chicken or
vegetable stock

1½ tbsp butter

⅓ cup flour

zest and juice of 1 orange

¼ tsp sugar

⅔ cup light cream
thin strips of orange zest

1   Pour the tomatoes and juice into a large saucepan with the onion, carrot, lemon and orange zests, bouquet garni, peppercorns, salt and stock.

2   Bring to a boil slowly, cover and allow to simmer gently for 30 minutes. Allow to cool slightly and purée in a food processor, blender or food mill.

3   Rinse the saucepan and melt the butter, add the flour and make a roux. Cook the roux for 3 minutes, then add the soup gradually with the orange juice and sugar.

4   Taste and adjust the seasoning, add three-quarters of the cream and gently reheat.

5   While the soup is cooking, cut thin strips of orange zest without pith. Blanch in boiling water for 3 minutes and drain. Use these to garnish the soup with a swirl of cream on top.

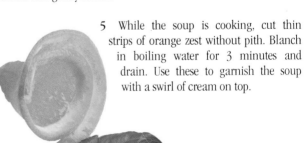

Zucchini Soup

1   Heat the oil in a large saucepan over a low heat. Add the onion and green onions. Allow to cook gently on a low heat, stirring frequently, until the onions are transparent.

2   Add the zucchini and potatoes to the onion and allow to brown slightly, stirring from time to time.

3   Add the tomatoes and stock, bring to a boil and allow to simmer for 15 minutes.

4   Throw in the pasta and allow the soup to cook in a more lively fashion for about 7-8 minutes until the pasta is al dente.

5   Serve sprinkled with grated nutmeg and chopped parsley.

VARIATION
Cream of Zucchini Soup
Omit the pasta from the soup and purée in a blender, food processor or food mill. Reheat the soup and serve with a spoonful of sour cream or yogurt on top of each serving.

INGREDIENTS

Serves 6

3 tbsp oil

1 onion, sliced

4 green onions, sliced

6 zucchini, diced

2 potatoes, sliced

12 plum tomatoes, peeled, or two 14½ oz cans

2 quarts stock

¼ pound small pasta shapes

¼ tsp nutmeg

1 tbsp parsley

17

Pauper's Soup

INGREDIENTS

Serves 4

1 French bread

2 garlic cloves, halved

4½ cups chicken stock

1 cup broccoli flowerets

1 cup cauliflower flowerets

½ cup grated cheese

1 Cut the French bread into thick slices. Rub the surfaces with the cut garlic cloves.

2 Heat the chicken stock and add the broccoli and cauliflower. Cook for about 5 minutes until tender.

3 Place the soup in warmed bowls and arrange 2 or 3 pieces of bread in each bowl. Sprinkle with grated cheese and serve.

Minestrone Milanese

1   Cut the bacon slices into small dice. Put the oil in a large saucepan on a low heat, add the bacon and cook gently for 1 minute.

2   Melt the butter in the pan, add the onion and fry for 2 minutes without browning. Add the carrots, celery, potatoes and half the stock; simmer for 30 minutes.

3   Add all the remaining vegetables (except any frozen ones) together with the bouquet garni and the basil. Pour in the remaining stock, bring to a boil and simmer for 20 minutes.

4   Taste and season if necessary. Add the pasta or rice to the soup and cook for about 10 minutes.

5   Add frozen vegetables and continue cooking for a further 10 minutes. Remove from the heat, cover with a lid and allow to stand for 5 minutes.

6   Mix well and garnish with grated Parmesan cheese. Serve with pistou if liked (see page 27).

INGREDIENTS

Serves 6

2 slices bacon
2 tbsp oil
2 tbsp butter

1 large onion
2 medium carrots
2 celery stalks
2 medium potatoes, diced

2 quarts stock

¼ cup navy beans, canned
1 zucchini,
2 small leeks, sliced
½ cup snap beans
½ cup peas, frozen or fresh

14½ oz can tomatoes
¼ small green cabbage
1 bouquet garni
4 basil leaves
⅓ cup small pasta or rice
Parmesan cheese, grated
Pistou (optional)

Red Bean Soup

INGREDIENTS

Serves 4

15¼ oz can red kidney
beans

1 tbsp oil

1 onion, chopped

1-2 garlic cloves, minced

1 tsp oregano

¼ tsp chili powder

14½ oz can tomatoes

2½ cups beef stock

salt and pepper

2 tbsp chopped parsley

1   Drain the kidney beans and rinse well.

2   Heat the oil in a large saucepan and cook the onion and garlic over a low heat for 2 minutes.

3   Add the kidney beans and mash slightly with a fork. Add the oregano, chili powder, tomatoes and stock. Bring to a boil, reduce the heat and simmer for 5 minutes.

4   Stir well to break down the tomatoes and then continue cooking for 10 minutes. Taste for seasoning and garnish with parsley.

Celery with Cheese Soufflé

1   Melt the butter in a large saucepan, add the celery and thinly sliced onions and cook over a low heat until golden.

2   Add the ale and stock; season if necessary. Bring to a boil, then simmer gently for 1 hour.

3   Heat the oven to 425 °F.

4   Meanwhile make the cheese sauce. Heat the butter and flour in a saucepan to make a pale roux. Gradually add the milk, stirring constantly until thick. Season to taste and allow to cool. Beat in the egg yolks and Cheddar cheese.

5   Toast the slices of French bread in the oven. Pour the hot soup into a large ovenproof serving bowl or into individual bowls. Top with slices of toasted French bread.

6   Fold the stiffly beaten egg whites into the sauce and spoon over the French bread. Bake for 15 minutes and serve immediately.

INGREDIENTS

Serves 4-6

½ cup butter

1 head celery, sliced
1 pound small onions

2 ½ cups ale

2 ½ cups beef stock

6 slices French bread

2 egg whites

For the cheese sauce

¼ cup butter

½ cup flour

2 cups milk

2 egg yolks

⅔ cup grated Cheddar cheese

Avgolemono Soup

INGREDIENTS

Serves 4-6

4½ cups well-flavored
chicken stock

½ cup risotto rice or
small pasta shapes

3 eggs, separated

juice of 1 lemon

salt and pepper

thin strips of lemon zest

1　Pour the stock into a large saucepan and bring to a boil. Add the rice or pasta shapes and cook for 10 minutes or until tender. Remove any scum that forms during cooking.

2　Beat the egg whites until white and fluffy. Gradually add the yolks and beat until light and creamy. When the mixture begins to thicken, add the lemon juice.

3　Beat about 1 cup of boiling soup into the egg mixture. Very gradually, add the remainder of the soup beating well all the time.

4　Adjust the seasoning to taste and serve immediately, garnished with a slice of lemon.

COOK'S TIP

For good flavor, it is better to use a homemade chicken stock for this soup rather than commercial cubes. The remainder of the preparation is very quick and must be done immediately before serving.

Tomato and Avocado Soup

1   Melt the butter in a saucepan, add the onion and fry gently without browning for a few minutes. Add the tomatoes, reserving the juice.

2   Cut 4 thin slices from the avocado and reserve for garnishing. Add the remaining avocado, stock, tomato juice, herbs and lemon juice to the pan. Bring to a boil and simmer for 15 minutes.

3   Blend the soup in a blender or food processor. Season to taste. Serve hot or chilled with a slice or two of avocado floating on top.

COOK'S TIP
To make a quick version of this soup, blend the tomatoes and avocado with the stock, lemon or lime juice and seasoning, add a few drops of hot-pepper sauce and serve chilled, garnished with sour cream.

INGREDIENTS

Serves 4

2 tbsp butter

1 onion, roughly chopped

14 ¼ oz can tomatoes

1-2 avocados, halved, seeded and peeled

4 ½ cups chicken stock

½ tsp oregano or chervil

juice of 1 lemon or lime

salt and pepper

Split-Pea Soup

INGREDIENTS

Serves 6

1 cup yellow split peas

4½ cups ham stock

2 potatoes, diced

2 carrots, diced

small bunch thyme or 1 bouquet garni

12 pearl onions

strips of carrot, to garnish

1   Soak the split peas for 2-3 hours. Drain well. Place in a large saucepan with the stock and simmer until tender over a low heat.

2   Add the potatoes, carrots and herbs, then bring to a boil and simmer until all the vegetables are tender.

3   Peel the onions and cook them in 1¼ cups boiling water until tender. Strain, retaining the cooking water.

4   Purée the soup in a food processor, blender or food mill. If it is too thick, add some of the onion water until you have a good soup consistency. Add the onions and reheat gently.

5   Serve with 2 or 3 onions in each portion, garnished with strips of carrot.

COOK'S TIP

To make this a complete meal, add 1 cup diced boiled ham. Reheat with the onions (step 4) before serving.

Country Vegetable Soup

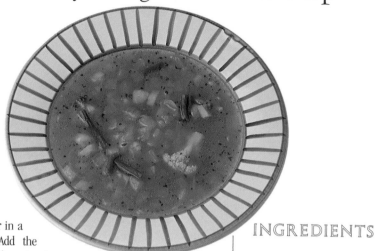

1 Melt the butter in a large saucepan. Add the onions, carrots, celery, turnip, parsnip and potato. Stir the vegetables in the butter until they are coated.

2 Add the stock, bring to a boil and simmer for 25 minutes.

3 Taste for seasoning, add the peas or beans and simmer for a further 10 minutes.

4 Serve in heated bowls sprinkled with chopped parsley.

COOK'S TIP
If using fresh peas and beans, allow 15 minutes cooking time in Step 3.

INGREDIENTS

Serves 6

¼ cup butter

2 onions, chopped

2-3 carrots, diced

3-4 celery stalks, thinly sliced

1 small new turnip, diced

1 parsnip, diced

1 medium potato, diced

6 cups chicken stock

salt and pepper

¼ pound frozen peas or snap beans

1 tbsp parsley, chopped

Indonesian Noodle Soup

INGREDIENTS

Serves 4-6

¼ pound fine egg noodles

6 cups chicken stock

8 green onions, 4 finely chopped

1 head broccoli, in small flowerets

1 large beefsteak tomato, skinned and chopped

1 tbsp soy sauce

1 tsp ground cumin

1 tsp ground coriander

¼ pound Chinese cabbage, shredded

1   Place the noodles in a bowl of hot water for a few minutes until the strands separate. Pour through a strainer.

2   Heat the stock in a large pan or wok. Add the green onions, broccoli, tomato, soy sauce, cumin and coriander. Bring to a boil and reduce the heat. Allow to simmer for about 5 minutes.

3   Add the Chinese cabbage, stir for 2 minutes, then add the egg noodles. Allow the soup to simmer for about 4 minutes or until the noodles are cooked.

4   Garnish with strips of onion or a green onion flower.

VARIATION
For a more substantial soup, add 1 cup thinly sliced cooked chicken, turkey or duck before adding the noodles.

Pistou Soup

1 Drain the navy beans. (If using dried, soak them overnight. Rinse and cook them in a large saucepan with 9 cups of water. Bring to a rolling boil for 10 minutes, then simmer for 3 hours.)

2 Add the carrots and turnip, then the potatoes, zucchini, leeks and sliced snap beans. Pour in the stock, bring to a boil and simmer gently for 1 hour. Stir occasionally to break up the larger pieces of vegetable.

3 Add the pasta and cook for 5 minutes.

4 Meanwhile, grate the Swiss cheese and then blend all the pistou ingredients or mash together in a bowl. Stir the mixture into the soup and reheat briefly. Basil leaves make an appropriate garnish.

COOK'S TIP
For a dinner party, it is better to serve the pistou mixture separately so guests can add it to taste.

INGREDIENTS

Serves 6

¼ pound navy beans

2 carrots, finely chopped

1 small turnip, diced

2 large potatoes, cubed

2 zucchini, sliced

2 large leeks, sliced

½ pound snap beans

2½ cups stock

⅓ cup small pasta

For the pistou

2 garlic cloves, minced
and 3 tbsp olive oil
4 sprigs basil or parsley

½ cup Swiss cheese

Curried Parsnip Soup

INGREDIENTS

Serves 4

2 tbsp butter

1 onion, finely chopped

1 carrot, grated

2 parsnips, finely chopped

2 tsp mild curry powder

generous ½ cup lentils

5 cups beef or vegetable stock

salt and pepper

fresh parsley or coriander

light cream (optional)

1   Melt the butter in a large saucepan. Add the onion, carrot and parsnips.

2   Stir around on a low heat until the vegetables are well coated with the butter.

3   Add the curry powder and mix well with the vegetables. Stir over a low heat for at least 2 minutes, then add the lentils, stock and seasoning.

4   Simmer on a medium to low heat (do not boil) for 30 minutes. Allow to stand for 10 minutes, then purée in a food processor, blender or food mill.

5   Serve garnished with coriander or parsley and a swirl of cream.

Potage Printanier

1   Cut the potatoes into even-sized pieces. Place in a large saucepan with the water, bring to a boil and simmer until cooked. Pour through a strainer, retaining the water.

2   Put the potatoes through a ricer or a coarse strainer (do not use a food processor).

3   Cook the carrots and fresh peas in the potato water for 5 minutes, then add the leek and frozen peas if using; cook for a further 3 minutes. Drain, reserving the liquid.

4   Add the bouillon cube to 2½ cups of the reserved liquid and pour onto the potatoes. Beat well until smooth, adding the butter and seasoning.

5   Add the peas and carrots and cook gently until tender.

6   Pour in the hot milk and nutmeg. Taste for seasoning and serve sprinkled with parsley or chives. If too thick, add a little more of the vegetable cooking liquid.

COOK'S TIP

This delicious warming soup can be made very quickly by using instant potato if time is short. Mixed frozen peas and carrots can also be used, but fresh vegetables improve the flavor.

INGREDIENTS

Serves 4

2¼ pounds potatoes, peeled

9 cups lightly salted water

1 cup diced young carrots

¼ pound fresh or frozen peas

½ small leek, finely chopped

1 chicken or vegetable bouillon cube

2 tbsp butter

salt and pepper

5½ cups milk, heated

pinch of nutmeg

1 tbsp chopped parsley

Tuscan Bean Soup

INGREDIENTS

Serves 6

⅔ cup black-eyed beans,
soaked overnight

2 onions, diced

4 celery stalks

2 potatoes, diced

2 carrots, diced

1 new turnip, diced

14½ oz can plum tomatoes

4 basil leaves

1 bouquet garni

4½ cups stock

1 leek, sliced

1 tbsp parsley and ¼ cup
grated cheese

1 Put the beans in a large saucepan of water and bring to a boil. Remove the scum from the top and simmer for 40 minutes or until almost tender.

2 Drain and return to the saucepan with the onions, celery, potatoes, carrots and turnip. Add the tomatoes, herbs and stock; season with pepper.

3 Tip in the leek when the other vegetables are firm but almost cooked. Simmer for another 5 minutes. Taste for seasoning and add salt if needed. Serve sprinkled with parsley and grated cheese.

Potage St. Germain

1   In a saucepan, add
the peas and the drained and
chopped sorrel to the beef stock.
Cook gently, stirring from time to time.

2   Season the soup when half cooked (frozen peas will take half
the time of fresh). When the peas are tender, purée in a blender,
food processor or food mill.

3   Arrange the croutons in the bottom of warmed soup bowls and
pour the soup over.

4   Sprinkle with Parmesan cheese.

COOK'S TIP
If sorrel is unobtainable, use spinach and add 2 tsp lemon juice to
the stock.

INGREDIENTS

Serves 4

¾ pound peas, fresh or
frozen

½ cup sorrel, washed

4½ cups beef stock

salt and pepper

2 in croutons

¼ cup grated Parmesan
cheese

Tomato and Red Pepper Soup

INGREDIENTS

Serves 4

2 tbsp butter

1 large onion, chopped
2 carrots, chopped

2½ cups vegetable stock

2 sprigs fresh basil
1 bay leaf

1 large or 2 small red
bell peppers

2¼ pounds plum
tomatoes

⅔ cup milk

⅔ cup light cream

1   Melt the butter in a large saucepan, then add the onion and carrots. Cook for 3-4 minutes, stirring occasionally.

2   Add the stock, basil and bay leaf, then cover and simmer for 10 minutes. Remove the seeds and core from the peppers. Cut into thin strips, retaining several for the garnish. Add the pepper strips with the tomatoes to the saucepan and simmer for 15 minutes.

3   Season with salt and black pepper and purée in a food processor, blender or food mill.

4   Add the milk with half the cream and reheat gently, ensuring the mixture doesn't boil.

5   Blanch the remaining pepper strips in boiling water for 4 minutes and use them as a garnish with the rest of the cream swirled on top of each serving.

Celery and Dill Soup

1   Melt the butter in a
large saucepan. Add the onion
and stir until evenly coated in butter.

2   Prepare the celery by removing the stringy bits with a potato
peeler and cutting into even-sized pieces. Add to the onion and stir
until the butter is absorbed.

3   Add all the remaining ingredients, bring to a boil and simmer
for about 30 minutes.

4   Purée in a blender, food processor or food mill, then return to
the saucepan and reheat until piping hot.

VARIATION
Cream of Celery Soup
Omit the dill seeds, and add ⅔ cup light cream after the soup has
been puréed. Serve hot with a garnish of chopped parsley or dill.

INGREDIENTS

Serves 4

¼ cup butter

2 onions, coarsely
chopped

2 heads celery

4½ cups chicken stock

salt and pepper

1 bouquet garni

1 tbsp sherry, optional

1 tbsp dried dill seed

Quick French Onion Soup

INGREDIENTS

Serves 4

¼ cup butter

1 pound onions, sliced

1 garlic clove, minced

1 tbsp all-purpose flour

4½ cups beef stock

1 tsp Worcestershire
sauce

1 sprig thyme

4-8 slices French bread

2 tsp French mustard

½ cup grated Swiss
cheese

fresh parsley

1   Melt the butter in a large saucepan without browning. Add the thinly sliced onion rings and garlic; cook on a medium heat until evenly golden brown.

2   After about 10 minutes sprinkle in the flour and allow to turn golden, stirring from time to time.

3   Gradually add the stock, stirring well. Add the Worcestershire sauce, seasoning and thyme. Simmer for 15-20 minutes, stirring from time to time.

4   Meanwhile spread the bread with the mustard, sprinkle with grated cheese and brown under the broiler.

5   Float the bread in the soup and garnish with parsley.

COOK'S TIP
Be very careful not to burn the onions – this would spoil the flavor of the soup.
    If more time is available, cook the bread and cheese in the oven at 350°F for 10 minutes. Place the bread and cheese on the bottom of an ovenproof dish and pour on the soup – the bread will rise to the top. Sprinkle with a little Parmesan cheese and cook at 400°F until bubbling.

Artichoke and Pasta Soup

1   Peel and dice the artichokes and then place them in a saucepan of water with the lemon juice. Bring to a boil and cook for 10 minutes on a medium heat. Drain into a strainer.

2   Cut the bacon into small dice. Place in a saucepan. Cook for 1 minute, then add the onion, garlic, green onions and tomatoes. Add the stock and tomato paste.

3   Bring to a boil, add the artichokes and simmer on a low heat for 10 minutes.

4   Throw in the pasta, stir well and cook for 10 minutes.

5   Taste and adjust the seasoning and serve garnished with Parmesan cheese and parsley.

INGREDIENTS

Serves 4

6 Jerusalem artichokes

juice of 1 lemon

3 slices bacon

1 medium onion, diced

1 garlic clove, minced

2 green onions, sliced

2 beefsteak tomatoes, peeled and chopped

4½ cups beef or ham stock

1 tbsp tomato paste

⅔ cup pasta shapes

2 tbsp grated Parmesan

1 tbsp chopped parsley

Lentil Soup

INGREDIENTS

Serves 4

2 tbsp oil or 2 tbsp butter

2 medium onions, finely chopped

3 cups grated carrot

2 celery stalks, finely chopped

⅔ cup red lentils

1 bay leaf

1 bouquet garni

5 cups beef or vegetable stock

salt and pepper

whole-wheat croutons (optional)

1   Heat the oil or butter (or a mixture of both) in a large saucepan. Add the onion and stir for about 1 minute, then add the carrot and celery. Cook on a low heat for about 4 minutes, turning the vegetables over from time to time.

2   Add the lentils to the pan with the herbs and stock. Stir well, bring to a boil and simmer, partially covered, for about 35-40 minutes.

3   Skim the surface from time to time as lentils tend to produce a frothy scum.

4   Taste for seasoning and serve garnished with slices of carrot. Toasted or fried whole-wheat croutons also make an excellent accompaniment.

Lentil and Tomato Soup

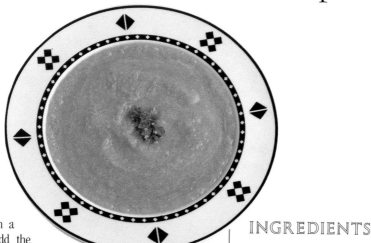

1   Heat the oil in a large saucepan, add the onion and stir for about 1 minute before adding the carrot and celery. Cook over a gentle heat for about 5 minutes, stirring occasionally.

2   Add the lentils, turnip, parsnip, tomatoes, herbs and stock to the saucepan. Bring to a boil, stirring continuously. Simmer with the pan partially covered for about 35-40 minutes. Skim the surface from time to time to remove any frothy scum.

3   Allow to cool slightly, then blend. Add a little extra stock or tomato juice if the soup is too thick.

4   Season and serve sprinkled with parsley.

VARIATION

Cream of Lentil and Tomato Soup
   Add ⅔ cup light cream at step 4, then garnish with fresh chopped parsley or coriander.

INGREDIENTS

Serves 4

2 tbsp oil

2 medium onions, finely chopped

3 cups grated carrot

2 celery stalks, finely chopped

½ cup red lentils

½ small turnip, chopped

1 parsnip, chopped

14½ oz can plum tomatoes

1 bouquet garni

5 cups vegetable stock

1 tbsp fresh parsley, chopped

Pumpkin and Ginger Soup

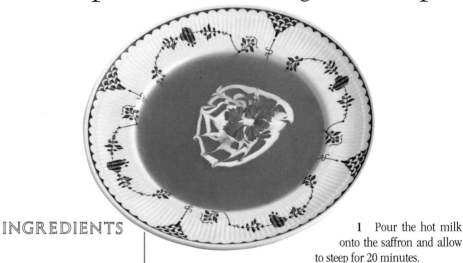

INGREDIENTS

Serves 4

⅔ cup hot milk

½ tsp saffron

¼ cup butter

2 onions, thinly sliced

2¼ pounds pumpkin flesh,
canned or fresh, cut into
even-sized pieces

1 tbsp sherry

4½ cups vegetable stock

1 small piece fresh ginger
root, peeled and chopped

salt and pepper

fresh parsley and light
cream, to garnish

1   Pour the hot milk onto the saffron and allow to steep for 20 minutes.

2   Heat the butter in a large saucepan and add the onions. Cook over a low heat until evenly coated – about 4-5 minutes.

3   Add the pumpkin to the onions and stir until coated – about a further 5 minutes.

4   Add the milk and saffron, sherry, stock, and ginger; simmer for at least 15 minutes. Taste for seasoning.

5   Purée in a blender or food mill and reheat until hot. Serve with a fresh leaf of parsley and a swirl of cream.

VARIATION
Pumpkin and Apple Soup
Use 1 pound pumpkin; 1 pound apples, quartered; ¼ tsp cinnamon; ⅔ cup cider and 4 cups stock. Cook as above, adding the apple and cinnamon with the pumpkin.

Cream of Tomato Soup

1   Melt the butter in a large saucepan. Add the onion and carrots and toss in the butter for about 3 minutes.

2   Add the stock, bouquet garni and basil. Simmer for 10 minutes, covered. Add the tomatoes and simmer for a further 15 minutes or until the carrots are tender.

3   Season and purée in a food processor, blender or food mill.

4   Add the milk and half the cream and reheat gently without boiling.

5   Serve with the remaining cream swirled on top of each portion and a few croutons.

INGREDIENTS

Serves 4

2 tbsp butter

1 large onion, chopped

2 carrots, chopped

2 ½ cups chicken or vegetable stock

bouquet garni

¼ tsp or 2 sprigs basil

2 ¼ pounds plum tomatoes or three 14 ½ oz cans plum tomatoes

salt and pepper

⅔ cup milk

⅔ cup light cream

garlic croutons

Spinach Soup

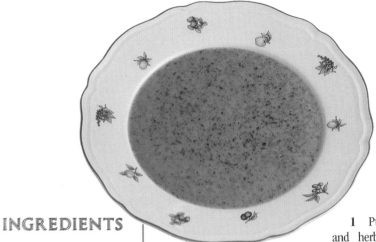

INGREDIENTS

Serves 6

2¼ pounds fresh spinach

outer leaves of 1 lettuce

3 green onions

3 large parsley sprigs

1 tsp chopped chives

½ tsp or 2 sprigs tarragon

¼ cup butter

salt and pepper

2 tsp cornstarch

4 cups stock

⅔ cup light cream

croutons and tarragon to
garnish (optional)

1   Put the vegetables and herbs in a blender. Cover with water and blend at high speed until they are all finely chopped. Transfer to a strainer to drain off the water.

2   Melt the butter in a large saucepan, add the vegetables and season to taste. Cook gently for a few minutes, stirring. Mix the cornstarch with a little water and hot soup. Return to the soup and beat in.

3   Add the stock, cover and cook for 15-20 minutes. Stir in the cream just before serving.

COOK'S TIP
For a smooth soup, purée the mixture and reheat gently without boiling. Garnish with croutons and fresh tarragon sprigs if available.

Asparagus Soup

1   Melt half the butter
in a saucepan, add the onion
and fry gently without browning for
a few minutes.

2   Add the asparagus, pour in the stock, season to taste and add
the chervil. Simmer for 25-30 minutes.

3   Blend the soup in a blender or food processor, or pass through
a food mill.

4   Heat the remaining butter in a saucepan on a low heat, stir in
the flour and cook for 2 minutes to make a pale roux. Gradually
add the milk, stirring constantly, then add the asparagus purée.

5   Bring to a boil and simmer for a few minutes. Taste and
adjust the seasoning and add 1 tbsp of the cream. Serve garnished
with a sprig of flat-leaved parsley and a swirl of cream.

COOK'S TIP
If you grow your own asparagus, this soup is an ideal way
of using up stems that have become large and coarse. If
using bought asparagus, use the tips
as an appetizer and make the soup
with the stalks. This
soup is also good
served chilled.

INGREDIENTS

Serves 4

2 tbsp butter

1 small onion, chopped

8–10 oz asparagus
scraped and roughly
chopped (keep 8 tips to
garnish)

1¼ cups chicken stock

salt and pepper

½ tsp chervil

1 tbsp flour

⅔ cup milk

2 tbsp whipping cream

fresh parsley

Cream of Artichoke Soup

INGREDIENTS

Serves 6

¼ cup butter

1 medium onion, sliced

2¼ pounds Jerusalem artichokes, peeled and sliced

1 potato, sliced

4½ cups chicken or vegetable stock

1 bay leaf

⅔ cup milk

salt and pepper

pinch of nutmeg

6 tbsp crème fraiche or sour cream

green onion, to garnish

1 Melt the butter in a large saucepan over a low heat. Add the onion and stir for 2 minutes. Tip in the artichoke and potato slices and stir for a further 2 minutes.

2 Add the stock and bay leaf. Cook for 20-30 minutes or until the vegetables are tender. Purée in a food processor, blender or food mill.

3 Return to the saucepan with the milk, crème fraiche or sour cream and seasonings. Serve garnished with strips of green onion.

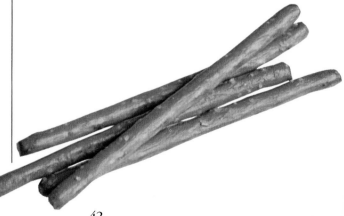

Cream of Celeriac Soup

1 If possible, prepare the vegetables in a food processor to cut the preparation time. Grate the celeriac.

2 Heat the butter in a large pan and toss the celeriac, potato and onion in it for about 2 minutes.

3 Add the leek and cook for a further 1 minute, then add the stock. Bring to a boil and simmer for 20 minutes or until the vegetables are tender. Purée the soup in a blender, food processor or food mill.

4 Mix the cornstarch with the milk and some of the hot soup; stir well. Pour into a pan with the remaining soup and heat, stirring, until slightly thickened. Check the seasoning.

5 Add the cream just before serving. Serve garnished with a sprig of parsley and grated cheese.

VARIATION
Celeriac and Mushroom Soup
Add 1 cup thinly sliced mushrooms after blending the soup and cook for 10 minutes.

INGREDIENTS

Serves 4

1 pound celeriac

¼ cup butter

1 large potato, sliced

1 small onion, sliced

1 leek, sliced

2½ cups chicken or vegetable stock

1 tbsp cornstarch

1¼ cups milk

salt and pepper

2 tbsp heavy cream

fresh parsley

2 tbsp grated Swiss cheese

Cream of Mushroom Soup

INGREDIENTS

Serves 4

5 cups mushrooms

¼ cup butter

1 small onion, diced

4½ cups chicken stock

1 bouquet garni

1 bay leaf

2 tbsp white wine

1 tbsp whole-wheat flour

salt and pepper

4 tbsp whipping cream

¼ tsp paprika

1   Retain two mushrooms for garnishing. Chop the remainder roughly. Heat half the butter in a large saucepan on a low heat.

2   Add the onion and cook for 3 minutes. Add the mushrooms and stir for a further 2 minutes.

3   Add the stock, bouquet garni, bay leaf and white wine. Bring to a boil and simmer for 15 minutes. Allow to cool slightly.

4   Blend the soup in a blender or food processor or pass through a food mill.

5   Heat the remaining butter in the cleaned saucepan and add the flour to make a roux. Cook for 1 minute, then gradually add the mushroom soup, stirring briskly. Season well.

6   Add 2 tbsp cream just before serving. Mix the remaining cream with the paprika.

7   Pour the soup into bowls and swirl the cream and paprika mixture on top. Garnish with raw mushroom slices.

Crème Dubarry

1   Break the cauliflower into flowerets and put in a large saucepan with the trimmed stem and potatoes. Pour in the stock and add a little salt. Bring to a boil and simmer, covered, until just tender.

2   Allow to cool slightly and purée in a blender, food processor or food mill.

3   Add the milk and nutmeg and bring slowly back to a boil, taste for seasoning. Serve if liked with a swirl of cream and some croutons.

INGREDIENTS

Serves 4

1 cauliflower, without green leaves

1 ¼ cups sliced potatoes

2 ½ cups chicken stock

salt and pepper

1 ¼ cups milk

½ tsp grated nutmeg

light cream (optional)

croutons

Blue Cheese Soup

INGREDIENTS

Serves 6

2 tbsp butter

1 medium onion, sliced

4 celery stalks, sliced

4½ cups vegetable or
chicken stock

3 cups thinly sliced
potatoes

salt and pepper

1 leek, thinly sliced

¼ pound blue cheese

chopped fresh chives

¼ tsp paprika

1 Melt the butter in a large saucepan, add the onion and cook over a low heat. Add the celery and stir for 1 minute.

2 Pour in the stock and add the potatoes. Season to taste, bring to a boil and simmer, covered, until the potatoes are almost cooked. Add the leek and cook for a further 10 minutes.

3 Allow to cool slightly, then purée in a food processor, blender or food mill with three-quarters of the cheese.

4 Reheat on a low heat. Serve in warmed bowls with a garnish of chopped chives and small cubes of the remaining cheese. Sprinkle with a little paprika.

Snow Pea Soup

1 Melt the butter in a large saucepan, add the oil and leave over a low heat. Add the onion and stir until well coated. Add the green onions. Cook for a further 3 minutes.

2 Sprinkle in the flour and stir into the onions. Allow to cook for about 2 minutes, stirring all the time. Gradually add the chicken stock, then the bay leaf and stir until smooth and thickened.

3 Add the peas (cut in half if they are large). Throw in the parsley and mint leaves. Bring to a boil and simmer for about 6-7 minutes, uncovered.

4 Purée the soup in a blender or food processor until fairly smooth.

5 Serve chilled, garnished with a swirl of cream and a few mint leaves on top.

INGREDIENTS

Serves 4

2 tbsp butter

1 tbsp olive oil

1 medium onion, diced

4 green onions, sliced

2 tbsp all-purpose flour

4 ¼ cups chicken stock

1 bay leaf

1 ¼ pounds snow peas, topped and tailed

2 tbsp chopped parsley

12 mint leaves

light cream and mint leaves

Lettuce Soup

INGREDIENTS

Serves 4

2 tbsp butter

1 onion, finely chopped

1 medium potato, finely sliced

2½ cups chicken or vegetable stock

1-2 lettuces, shredded

1 tbsp fresh chervil

1¼ cups milk

salt and pepper

4 tbsp crème fraîche

1   Melt the butter in a saucepan, add the onion and potato and cook gently for a few minutes over a low heat without browning.

2   Add the stock and simmer for 15 minutes.

3   Meanwhile poach the lettuce in the milk for about 10 minutes.

4   Add the lettuce, chervil and milk to the stock, season and cook for a further 5 minutes.

5   Blend the soup in a blender or food processor, then add 2 tbsp crème fraîche.

6   Reheat if serving hot, or chill in the refrigerator if serving cold.

7   Serve topped with a swirl of crème fraîche.

COOK'S TIP
This soup is ideal for using up leftover lettuce or a surplus from the garden – even bolted lettuces will do perfectly well, provided they are not bitter. The secret of a good flavor is to use enough lettuce.

Watercress Soup

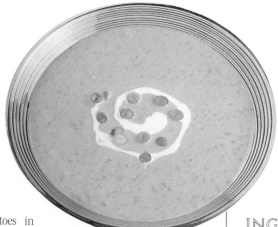

1 Cook the potatoes in the stock, with seasoning if needed, for about 10 minutes. Add the green onions and cook until the potatoes are soft.

2 Wash the watercress thoroughly and remove the leaves from the thick stems. Retain a few small sprigs for garnishing.

3 Add the watercress to the potatoes with the milk and chervil. Simmer over a low heat for about 10-15 minutes.

4 Purée the soup in a blender, food processor or food mill. Add half the cream and stir well before chilling in the refrigerator. Serve swirled with the remaining cream and garnished with watercress.

VARIATION
This watercress soup is equally good served hot.

INGREDIENTS

Serves 4

1 pound potatoes, cut into even pieces

2 ½ cups chicken stock

salt and pepper

3 green onions, chopped

3 bunches watercress

1 ¼ cups milk

2 tsp fresh or 1 tsp dried chervil

4 tbsp light cream

Spicy Avocado Soup

INGREDIENTS

Serves 4

4 ripe avocados, peeled

3 cups chicken stock

⅔ cup dry white wine

6 tbsp whipping cream

2 tbsp lemon juice

salt and pepper

few drops hot-pepper
sauce

1 Slice four rings of avocado and save for garnishing. Remove the seed and add the remaining flesh to a blender or food processor, then purée.

2 Add the stock, wine and cream gradually to the blender or processor, and purée together. Pour some of the lemon juice on the avocado garnish and add the remainder to the soup with seasoning to taste.

3 Chill and serve garnished with reserved avocado.

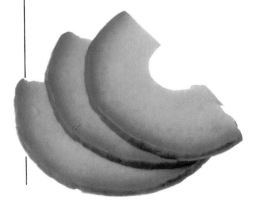

Chilled Cucumber Soup

1 Melt the butter in a large saucepan, add the onion and the chopped white part of the green onions (reserve the tops for garnishing). Stir over a low heat until the onions are soft and transparent but not brown.

2 Add the flour and cook until well absorbed by the butter; about 1½ minutes.

3 Add the stock and cucumber, bring to a boil and then cover and simmer for about 30 minutes.

4 Strain and blend in a food processor, blender or food mill. Season and add the lemon juice.

5 Cool, then chill in the refrigerator. Garnish with a swirl of cream and small squares of thinly sliced cucumber.

INGREDIENTS

Serves 4

¼ cup butter

1 large onion, diced

4 green onions

2 tbsp flour

4½ cups vegetable stock

2 cucumbers, diced

salt and pepper

juice of 1 lemon

1¼ cups light cream

Gazpacho

INGREDIENTS

Serves 6

2 slices bread

4 cups broth or water

2 tbsp wine vinegar

2 garlic cloves, minced

1 red onion, chopped

½ cucumber, sliced

4 tomatoes, skinned

2 red bell peppers

4 tbsp oil

To garnish

1 green bell pepper,
¼ cucumber and
2 tomatoes

4 tbsp small croutons

1   Soak the bread in a little of the stock or water.

2   Put the soaked bread, vinegar, garlic, onion, cucumber, tomatoes and roughly chopped peppers in a blender or food processor and reduce to a paste.

3   Gradually mix in the oil on slow speed, season to taste, then slowly add the rest of the stock or water, switching the machine on and off several times. Chill for several hours.

4   Cut the garnishing vegetables into tiny dice and serve separately, arranged in three rows on a serving plate or in individual bowls. Serve the croutons in a separate dish.

5   Serve the chilled soup in attractive bowls with 2 or 3 ice cubes.

COOK'S TIP
Use ripe plum or beefsteak tomatoes for a good color and flavor. Canned plum tomatoes are better than mild-flavored salad tomatoes.

For a special party soup, prepare the ice cubes with some tiny diced bell pepper and a sprig of parsley.

Melon and Cucumber Soup

1 Blend the melon flesh, 3 sprigs of mint and the cucumber in a blender or food processor until smooth. If liked, strain through a wide-meshed strainer to remove all seeds.

2 Mix with lemon juice and paprika. Chill in the refrigerator.

3 Serve garnished with ice cubes and mint sprigs.

COOK'S TIP
For a dinner party, add a few mint sprigs to the ice before freezing.

INGREDIENTS

Serves 4

1 ripe honeydew or canteloupe melon, peeled and seeded

3 mint sprigs

2 large cucumbers, peeled

3 tbsp lemon juice

¼ tsp paprika

extra mint sprigs to garnish

Vichyssoise

INGREDIENTS

Serves 4

2 onions

1 pound potatoes

¼ cup butter

4½ cups chicken stock

few sprigs parsley or chervil

1 bay leaf

salt and pepper

3 leeks

⅔ cup sour cream

1 tbsp chopped chives, parsley or green onion tops

1   Cut the vegetables into small even-sized pieces if the soup is to be served without puréeing. For a smooth soup, chop them roughly to save time.

2   Melt the butter in a heavy saucepan, add the onions and cook over a low heat for about 3 minutes. Gradually toss in the potatoes and stir until they have a coating of butter.

3   Pour in the chicken stock and add the herbs and seasoning. Bring to a boil and allow to cook for 10 minutes over a medium heat. Add the leeks and cook for a further 10 minutes.

4   Adjust the seasoning and make sure the potatoes are just tender. Remove the herb sprigs and bay leaf. Cool, stir in the sour cream, then chill until ready to serve.

5   Garnish with chives, parsley or green onion tops.

VARIATION
Cream of Leek and Potato Soup
In Step 5, stir in ⅔ cup light cream and pour into a blender or food processor. Blend until fairly smooth, reheat gently and serve immediately in warmed bowls. Garnish with a swirl of cream or leek rings.

Apple and Fennel Soup

1   Melt the butter in a large saucepan over a low heat. Add the onion, apples and fennel. Stir around in the pan until the vegetables are evenly coated and cook for about 4-5 minutes.

2   Pour in the stock, add the chives and simmer for about 30 minutes.

3   Allow to cool, then purée in a blender or food processor. Stir in 6 tbsp yogurt and chill in the refrigerator. Garnish with fronds of fennel, if available.

INGREDIENTS

Serves 4

¼ cup butter

2 onions, sliced

4 green apples, cored and peeled

1 fennel bulb, sliced

2½ cups chicken stock

1 tbsp chopped chives

6 tbsp plain yogurt

fennel fronds (optional)

Mediterranean Fish Soup

INGREDIENTS

Serves 8

2¼ pounds mussels
1 pound monkfish

1 bouquet garni

6 tbsp olive oil

2 celery stalks, sliced
2 onions, chopped
1 carrot, diced
2 garlic cloves'

14 oz plum tomatoes

2 tbsp wine vinegar

¼ tsp saffron

⅔ cup shelled shrimp

1 pound squid, prepared
8 cooked mussels and
shrimp in shells
to garnish

1 Scrub the mussels if necessary and remove any beards. Discard any which do not close when tapped with a knife.

2 Skin and bone the monkfish and cut into even-sized pieces.

3 In a large saucepan, bring 4½ cups of water or half water and half white wine to a boil. Add the bouquet garni and the mussels and cover. Shake occasionally, cook for 4-5 minutes.

4 Place a strainer over a bowl and drain the mussels, retaining the liquid in the bowl. Discard any unopened mussels.

5 Dry out the pan with a paper towel and place on a low heat. Pour in the oil and heat for 2 minutes, then add the onion.

6 Add the celery, carrot and garlic with the tomatoes. Pour in 1¼ cups water and simmer for 10 minutes.

7 Add the mussel liquid, vinegar, saffron and monkfish; stir gently. Season to taste and simmer for at least 10 minutes.

8 If liked, remove most of the shells from the mussels.

9 Add the prepared squid, cut into thin rings, and simmer for a further 4 minutes. Then add the mussels and shrimp.

Cullen Skink

1   Place the smoked haddock in a large saucepan with enough boiling water to cover.

2   Add the onion and simmer slowly until the fish is lightly cooked. Carefully lift out the fish and remove any bones; flake the flesh. Return the fish to the liquid and cook for 10 minutes.

3   Strain the fish liquid into a bowl and rinse the pan. Heat the milk in the pan on a low heat.

4   Add the butter and half the mashed potato. Season and mix well. Add the stock and the fish; stir carefully while heating.

5   Add more mashed potato a little at a time until a good thick soup consistency is obtained.

INGREDIENTS

Serves 4

1 smoked finnan haddock
or 2 large boned smoked
haddock

1 medium onion, chopped

2½ cups milk

2 tbsp butter

1 pound potatoes, boiled
and mashed

salt and pepper

a sprig of dill, to garnish

Manhattan Clam Chowder

INGREDIENTS

Serves 4

12-24 fresh or frozen
clams or 1 10 oz can

⅔ cup white wine

1 bouquet garni

4 slices bacon

2 tbsp butter

1 medium onion, diced
1 leek, chopped
1 green bell pepper,
deseeded
1 celery stalk, chopped
1 small potato, diced

½ tsp or 2 sprigs thyme
4-6 fresh tomatoes
1¼ cups tomato juice

fresh parsley

8 saltine crackers,
crushed

1   Poach clams for about 10 minutes in the white wine and 1¼ cups water with the bouquet garni. If using canned clams, poach for 5 minutes. Set aside.

2   Cut the bacon into small pieces. Melt the butter in a saucepan, add the bacon and fry gently for about 2 minutes.

3   Add the onion, leek, green pepper, celery and potato. Fry gently for about 6 minutes without browning.

4   Add the clam liquid along with seasoning to taste, thyme, chopped tomatoes and tomato juice.

5   Add 2 cups water, bring to a boil and simmer until the vegetables are tender.

6   Add the clams a few minutes before serving, sprinkled with finely chopped parsley and crushed crackers.

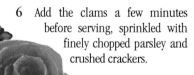

Spicy Indonesian Soup

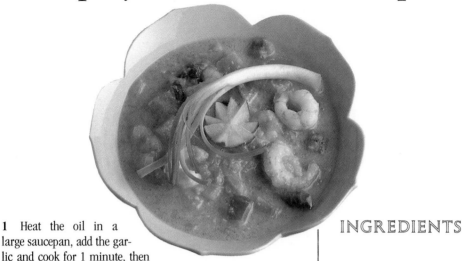

1 Heat the oil in a large saucepan, add the garlic and cook for 1 minute, then add the green onion, chili and lemon grass. Stir for a minute, then pour in the stock.

2 Add the pumpkin and mix well. Simmer for 20 minutes.

3 Make up the creamed coconut with ⅔ cup warm water. Add to the soup with the basil. Break down the ingredients with a potato masher, or for a smooth soup purée in a blender or food processor.

4 Add the shrimp and reheat slowly over a low heat without boiling. Garnish with green-onion flowers.

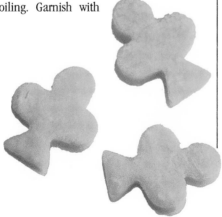

INGREDIENTS

Serves 4

1 tbsp vegetable oil

1-2 garlic cloves, minced

4 green onions, chopped

1 red chili, deseeded

1 tbsp lemon grass, chopped

4½ cups chicken stock

1½ pounds pumpkin flesh, canned or fresh, diced

¼ pound creamed coconut

1 tbsp shredded basil

¼ pound cooked shrimp, shelled

green-onion flowers

Quick Crab Soup

INGREDIENTS

Serves 4

1 large crab or 2 small,
boiled

2½ cups fish stock

scant ¼ cup risotto rice

salt and pepper

1 bay leaf

1 bouquet garni

2½ cups milk

⅔ cup whipping cream

½ tsp anchovy paste

1 tsp tomato paste

fresh parsley

1   Remove the brown and white meat from the crab. Retain the claw meat for garnishing.

2   Bring the stock to a boil and sprinkle in the rice. Cook, stirring, for 5 minutes. Cover and leave on a low heat until tender.

3   Purée in a blender or food processor and return to the pan with seasoning, bay leaf, bouquet garni and crab meat and milk. Heat slowly without allowing the soup to boil.

4   Add the cream, anchovy paste and tomato paste and mix well. Stir in the claw meat, remove bouquet garni, and serve sprinkled with parsley.

COOK'S TIP
Frozen crab makes an excellent soup when fresh crabs are unavailable. Buy 1 pound – there is no need to defrost it first, providing it is reheated until completely defrosted. Use some defrosted white meat to garnish.

Bouillabaisse

1   Use the trimmings from the fish to make a Court Bouillon (see page 8). Cook for only 15 minutes as overcooked fish liquid becomes bitter.

2   Heat the oil in a large pan, add the vegetables, garlic, thyme, orange and lemon zests, saffron and seasoning and stir around until coated in oil. Add the strained fish liquid. Cook for 15 minutes.

3   Add the pieces of fish, but retain fresh or defrosted shellfish until nearer serving. Cook for 10 minutes. Add the shellfish and saffron and cook for a further 10 minutes. Taste and adjust the seasoning.

4   Line soup plates with the French bread and ladle the soup on top. Garnish with parsley and the jumbo shrimp.

INGREDIENTS

Serves 6

2 pounds fish and shell-fish (cod, hake, whiting, mullet, crayfish, mussels, shrimp)

2 tbsp olive oil
2 onions, diced
2 carrots, sliced
1 red bell pepper
6 plum tomatoes
1 bunch parsley
2 celery stalks, chopped
2 garlic cloves, minced
2 green onions or shallots, sliced
1 sprig thyme
zest of 1 orange and 1 lemon

¼ tsp saffron

warmed French bread

jumbo shrimp

New England Clam Chowder

INGREDIENTS

Serves 4

12-24 clams or 1 10 oz can

⅔ cup white wine

1 bay leaf
1 bouquet garni

¼ pound bacon

2 tbsp butter

1 medium onion, diced

2 leeks, chopped

2 celery stalks, chopped

2 small potatoes, diced

2 sprigs or ½ tsp thyme

⅔ cup milk
4 tbsp light cream

fresh parsley

1   Poach the clams for about 10 minutes in the white wine and ⅔ cup water with bay leaf and bouquet garni. If using canned clams, poach for 5 minutes. Set aside.

2   Cut the bacon into small pieces. Melt the butter in a saucepan, add the bacon and fry gently for about 2 minutes.

3   Add the onion, leeks, celery and potato. Fry gently for about 6 minutes without browning.

4   Add the clam liquid along with seasoning and the thyme.

5   Add 1¼ cups water, bring to a boil and simmer gently until the vegetables are tender. Add the milk and simmer for 4 minutes.

6   Add the clams and cream a few minutes before serving, garnished with fresh parsley.

Shrimp Bisque

1   Remove the shrimp from the shells and simmer the shells in the Court Bouillon with the carrot, onion, parsley and seasoning for 30 minutes. Strain the stock into a bowl.

2   Melt the butter in a saucepan and add the flour to make a pale roux. Gradually beat in the shrimp liquid, bring to a boil and cook for about 5 minutes.

3   Add most of the shrimp, retaining 4 to garnish. Stir in the lemon juice, cream and sherry; heat gently without boiling. Taste and adjust the seasoning.

4   Serve with a shrimp on each portion.

VARIATION
Lobster Bisque
Use one cooked hen lobster. Remove the meat and cut into neat pieces. Serve with lobster butter made by pounding 1 tbsp lobster coral with 2 tbsp butter.

INGREDIENTS

Serves 4

1 pound whole shrimp

4½ cups Court Bouillon (page 8)

1 carrot

1 onion, sliced

large parsley sprig

salt and pepper

2 tbsp butter

¼ cup all-purpose flour

juice of ½ lemon

⅔ cup light cream

4 tbsp sherry

shrimp to garnish

Chilean Fish Soup

INGREDIENTS

Serves 6

3 tbsp olive oil

2 onions, finely chopped

1 small red bell pepper
and 1 small green bell
pepper

2 carrots, thinly sliced

1 tsp paprika

2 ¼ pounds potatoes

1 bay leaf
½ tsp or 1 sprig oregano
3 sprigs parsley

6 cups fish stock

2 ¼ pounds cod or bass,
filleted

4 oz shelled shrimp

1   Heat the oil in a flameproof casserole or heavy-based saucepan. Add the onions and stir over a low heat until transparent but not brown; about 5 minutes.

2   Add deseeded and diced bell peppers and the carrots and stir well on a medium heat. Sprinkle with paprika.

3   Add peeled and diced potatoes, the bay leaf, oregano, parsley and fish stock. Simmer for at least 15 minutes, but do not boil or the stock will become bitter.

4   Add the fish and cook over a low heat, covered, for at least 10 minutes. Remove the bay leaf and parsley. Add shrimp.

5   Serve in a heated dish or soup bowls.

COOK'S TIP
A garnish of ⅔ cup cooked shrimp or coriander may be added.

Oxtail Soup

1 Heat the oil in a saucepan and brown the oxtail joints in it. Chop up all the vegetables, add them to the saucepan and cook until golden.

2 Add the stock or water, bring to a boil and add the herbs and seasoning. Simmer for 1½ hours, skimming the surface frequently to remove scum.

3 Take out the oxtail and leave the soup until quite cold. Meanwhile, remove the meat from the oxtail and discard the bones.

4 Skim the fat from the cold soup. Heat the butter and flour together to make a brown roux, then gradually add the skimmed soup, beating until well mixed and slightly thickened.

5 Add the sherry and simmer for 15 minutes. Taste and adjust the seasoning; add the oxtail pieces. Sprinkle with chopped parsley.

INGREDIENTS

Serves 4-6

2 tbsp oil

1 oxtail, cut into joints

2 medium onions

1 celery stalk

1 carrot

½ cup chopped turnip

9 cups stock or water

1 bay leaf

¼ tsp Italian seasoning

¼ cup butter

½ cup flour

4 tbsp sherry

1 tbsp chopped parsley

Chicken Broth

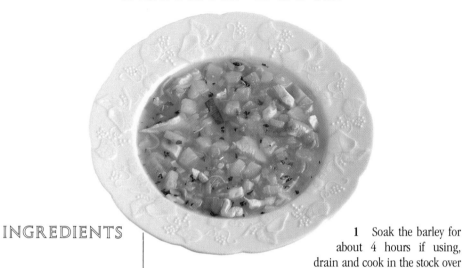

INGREDIENTS

Serves 4

¼ cup pearl barley
(opional)

5 cups chicken stock

2 tbsp butter

2 onions, finely chopped

3 celery stalks, finely
chopped

2 medium carrots, diced

1 small new turnip, diced

1 bouquet garni

salt and pepper

2 leeks, trimmed and
sliced

1½ cups diced cooked
chicken

1 Soak the barley for about 4 hours if using, drain and cook in the stock over a medium heat for about 30 minutes.

2 Melt the butter in a skillet over a low heat. Add the onion and cook for about 3 minutes, turning from time to time. Add the celery, carrots and turnip, cook for a further 2 minutes.

3 Add the vegetables to the barley and stock with the bouquet garni and salt and pepper. Simmer over a medium heat for 30 minutes then add the leeks.

4 Cook for a further 5 minutes, then add the chicken. Simmer for a further 10 minutes, stirring at least twice. Remove the bouquet garni and taste for seasoning.

5 Serve piping hot, generously sprinkled with chopped parsley.

VARIATION
For chicken broth without barley, cook the vegetables as in step 2. The stock does not require to be heated before adding the vegetables. Rice may be used in place of barley. The rice would be added with the vegetables to the stock in step 3.

Cream of Chicken Soup

1   Melt the butter, add the onion and cook on a low heat for 2 minutes.

2   Sprinkle in the flour and stir in with a wooden spoon for about 2 minutes; do not allow to brown.

3   Gradually add the stock, beating to avoid lumps. Add the bay leaf, bouquet garni and seasonings. Bring to a boil, beating all the time, and simmer for 15 minutes.

4   Add the milk and mix well. Tip in the chicken and cook for a further 20 minutes without boiling. Remove the bay leaf and bouquet garni.

5   Serve garnished with croutons and parsley for color.

VARIATION
For extra flavor and color, cook ⅔ cup sliced mushrooms and ½ finely diced red bell pepper with the onion in step 1. Add ½ cup frozen peas in step 4. No further garnish is needed.

INGREDIENTS

Serves 4

¼ cup butter

1 onion, diced

2 tbsp all-purpose flour

2 ¼ cups chicken stock, warmed

1 bay leaf

1 bouquet garni

salt and pepper

pinch of nutmeg

1 ¼ cups milk

⅔ cup finely diced cooked chicken

croutons and parsley sprigs

Scotch Broth

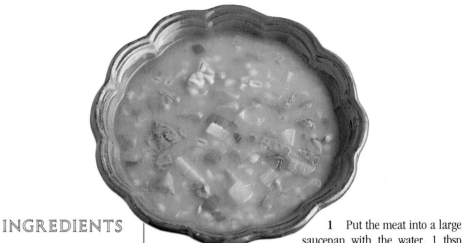

INGREDIENTS

Serves 4-6

1 pound stewing lamb
chops, trimmed

4½ cups water

salt and pepper

1 bay leaf

½ cup pearl barley

¼ cup dried peas, soaked

2 carrots, diced

1 large onion, cut into
rings

1 small turnip, diced

3 leeks, sliced

1 Put the meat into a large saucepan with the water, 1 tbsp salt, pepper to taste and the bay leaf. Add the pearl barley and peas. Bring to a boil and simmer for 1 hour. Remove the meat with a slotted spoon and cut into small pieces.

2 Add the carrots, onion and turnip to the cooking liquid and simmer for 15 minutes.

3 Skim any fat that has risen to the surface of the broth. Add the leeks, return the meat to the soup and cook for 10 minutes.

4 Skim any fat from the surface with paper towels.

COOK'S TIP
This is an excellent soup for a nourishing, economical snack meal. It is best cooked a day ahead and allowed to cool in the refrigerator. The fat can then be lifted off the surface without having to skim the soup during cooking.

Cabbage Soup with Meatballs

1   Melt the butter in a large saucepan over a low heat. Add the onion and green onions and cook gently until transparent.

2   Add the stock, tomato juice, seasonings and rice. Bring to a boil and simmer for 15 minutes.

3   Meanwhile, make the meatballs (see below) and put in the refrigerator.

4   Add the cabbage to the soup and cook for 10-15 minutes until done to taste.

5   Add the meatballs and cook for a further 10 minutes.

COOK'S TIP
Meatballs can be added to many vegetable soups to make a complete snack meal. Mix ¼ pound lean ground beef or pork with 1 tbsp bread crumbs, 1 finely chopped green onion, ½ tsp Italian seasoning, salt, pepper, ¼ tsp apple-pie spice, pinch of paprika and 1 tbsp yogurt or cream. Make into 12 small balls and roll between lightly floured hands. Chill in the refrigerator for about 15 minutes before using.

INGREDIENTS

Serves 6

¼ cup butter

1 onion, diced

2 green onions, sliced

5 cups beef stock

1 ¼ cups tomato juice

½ tsp apple-pie spice

salt and pepper

scant ¼ cup long-grain rice

8 ½ cups finely shredded white and green cabbage

12 meatballs

Green Pea and Ham Soup

INGREDIENTS

Serves 6

1 small ham, soaked
overnight

1½ onions, diced

2 bouquets garni

1 bay leaf

8 peppercorns

2 cups dried peas, soaked
overnight

2 tbsp butter

2 celery stalks, sliced

1 carrot, sliced thinly

black pepper

⅔ cup light cream

1   Rinse the ham several times and place in a saucepan with ½ onion, 1 bouquet garni, the bay leaf and peppercorns. Cover with water, bring to a boil and simmer for 20 minutes for each 1 pound and 20 minutes extra. Top up with boiling water as needed and skim twice at the beginning of cooking. Remove the ham to a plate and strain the stock.

2   Drain the peas and rinse thoroughly. Place in a saucepan with 6 cups of the ham stock. Bring to a boil and cook on a rolling boil for 10 minutes. Reduce the heat and simmer, covered, for 30 minutes, stirring occasionally.

3   Melt the butter in a skillet and add the remaining onion; stir for 2 minutes. Add the celery and carrot and cook for 3 minutes, stirring occasionally.

4   Add to the peas with the remaining bouquet garni. Season with black pepper and simmer for 30 minutes.

5   Allow to cool slightly, remove bouquet garni and bay leaf, then purée in a food processor, blender or a food mill. Reheat with the cream, without boiling.

6   Cut one slice of ham into small cubes and add to the soup. Serve in warm bowls with the remaining cream swirled on top.

Mexican Soup

1   Dry-fry the ground beef over a medium heat in a non-stick skillet. Break the meat down into small pieces with a wooden spoon or fork, turning frequently until well browned.

2   Tip the meat into a large saucepan and use the fat left in the skillet to cook the onion and garlic. If very little is left, add some oil. Fry them for about 3 minutes. Add the chili pepper and stir.

3   Mix the chili powder with some of the tomato liquid and pour onto the vegetables. Cook for another 2 minutes.

4   Add to the meat with the tomatoes. Rinse out the skillet with the beef stock. Bring to a boil, breaking down the tomatoes with a spoon.

5   Simmer the mixture for 15 minutes, then add the kidney beans and corn. Season and simmer for a further 15-20 minutes. Serve garnished with chili flowers or parsley sprigs and accompanied by taco chips.

INGREDIENTS

Serves 4

½ pound ground beef

2 onions, diced

1 garlic clove, minced

1 chili pepper, deseeded and chopped

1 tsp chili powder

two 14½ oz cans plum tomatoes

¼ cup beef stock

14½ oz can red kidney beans

4 tbsp whole-kernel corn and baby corn cobs

1 tbsp chopped parsley

parsley sprigs

Feather Fowlie

INGREDIENTS

Serves 6

4 chicken joints

1 slice raw ham or lean bacon

1 bouquet garni

1 onion, sliced

2 celery stalks, sliced

salt and pepper

1 chicken bouillon cube

3 egg yolks

3 tbsp light cream, warmed

celery leaves

1   Place the chicken joints in a bowl covered with salted water and allow to steep for 30 minutes. Rinse with cold water.

2   Put the joints into a large saucepan with the ham or bacon, bouquet garni, onion, celery and seasoning. Cover with water and crumble in the chicken bouillon cube. Bring to a boil and simmer gently for about 1 hour.

3   Strain the stock into a bowl and allow to cool, then refrigerate. Remove solidified fat from the surface. Finely chop about 1½ cups of chicken meat.

4   Mix the egg yolks with the cream. Heat the chicken stock with the chopped chicken. Add a little of the hot stock to the egg mixture, then carefully add to the soup. Do not boil.

5   Serve in warm bowls and garnish with a celery top.

COOK'S TIP
Use the remainder of the chicken and the ham diced in a parsley sauce or in a chicken and ham pot pie. Alternatively, make chicken and ham croquettes.

Thai Chicken Soup

1 Slice the chicken breasts into ½ in slices and set aside.

2 Heat the garlic, turmeric and cumin in a large saucepan for about 1 minute until the flavors have mingled.

3 Add the chicken, chicken stock, sugar and shrimp paste and simmer for 10 minutes.

4 Toss the rice vermicelli into the soup and cook for a further 10 minutes.

5 Just before serving add the bean sprouts and shredded leaves. Simmer for 2 minutes and sprinkle with coriander.

COOK'S TIP
Make this soup in advance up to step 4. Reheat on the stove or in the microwave and then add the bean sprouts, shredded leaves and coriander as in step 5.

INGREDIENTS

Serves 4-6

½ pound chicken breast

1 garlic clove, minced

¼ tsp turmeric

2 tsp ground cumin

6 cups chicken stock

1 tsp sugar

½ tsp shrimp paste

2 oz rice vermicelli

⅓ cup bean sprouts

3 Chinese leaves or lettuce leaves, shredded

1 tbsp chopped coriander

Cock-a-leekie

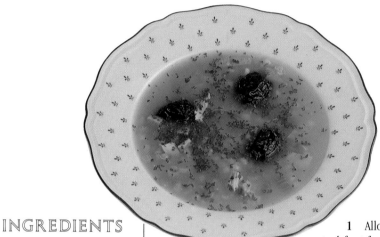

INGREDIENTS

Serves 6

4½ pound frozen chicken

½ lemon

2 onions, cut into wedges

6 celery stalks, chopped

6 small leeks

2 bay leaves

1 bouquet garni

6 peppercorns

2 slices pork belly or
piece of bacon

1½ cups pearl barley

8 no-soak dried prunes

1 tsp chopped parsley

1   Allow the chicken to defrost for at least 24 hours (or use the microwave oven). Wash the chicken thoroughly.

2   Half fill a large saucepan with water, add the lemon, onions, celery, 4 leeks, bay leaf, bouquet garni and peppercorns, then bring to a boil. Add the chicken with breast uppermost and make sure the legs are covered with the water.

3   Cut the rind from the pork and dice the meat. Add to the saucepan with the barley, cover and simmer for about 1 hour.

4   Remove the chicken to a plate; pour the liquid and vegetables into a bowl. Remove and discard the vegetables. Skim off the fat and return to a saucepan. Slice the remaining leeks and cook in the broth with the prunes for about 15 minutes.

5   Cut small slices of chicken and place in heated soup dishes. Ladle on the chicken broth and sprinkle with parsley.

COOK'S TIP
This is an excellent way of preparing several meals at the same time. The chicken can be served in a sauce as a main course. Any left over can be used in pot pies and vol-au-vent cases or served cold with salad and a spicy mayonnaise.

Devil's Soup

1 Put ham or vegetable stock in a large saucepan with the onions, garlic, chopped ham and mortadella sausage.

2 When the liquid returns to a boil, tear the spinach into strips, removing the stems and toss into the saucepan. Turn down the heat and simmer for 10 minutes.

3 Add the parsley, basil, pasta, peas and brandy. Simmer until the pasta and peas are tender.

4 Stir in the cream; remove the bunch of parsley and basil.

5 Serve in heated bowls sprinkled with grated Parmesan cheese.

INGREDIENTS

Serves 4

9 cups stock

2 onions, chopped

2 garlic cloves, minced

½ pound cooked ham

½ pound mortadella sausage, chopped

4 cups spinach

small bunch of parsley

4 basil leaves

1 ⅓ cups pasta shapes

¼ pound frozen peas

3 tbsp brandy

⅔ cup light cream
Parmesan cheese, grated

Quick Pea and Ham Soup

INGREDIENTS

Serves 4

1 potato, roughly chopped

1 onion, roughly chopped

1 pound frozen peas

4½ cups ham stock

salt and pepper

½ cup chopped cooked ham

1 Put the potato, onion and peas into a large saucepan with the ham stock. Bring to a boil and simmer for about 20 minutes.

2 Blend the soup in a food processor or blender. Taste and adjust the seasoning.

3 Add the ham and reheat briefly.

Mulligatawny Soup

1   Melt the butter in a saucepan and add the onion, carrot, peeled and chopped tomatoes, deseeded and chopped green pepper, celery and apple. Toss the ingredients in the butter for about 2 minutes.

2   Sprinkle in the curry powder and stir into the vegetables for another 2 minutes. Add the cloves, parsley, coriander, tomato paste, stock and a pinch of sugar. Season to taste, mix well and bring to a boil. Turn the heat down and simmer for 30 minutes.

3   Strain the soup or purée in a blender or food processor.

4   Mix the cornstarch with the milk. Add some of the hot soup, stir well and return to the pan. Stir until the soup is thickened. Add the chicken and cooked rice; reheat for 5 minutes.

5   Garnish with coriander and serve with poppadums.

VARIATION
This soup can also be made using 1 pound cubed shin of beef or stewing lamb. Fry the onion in the oil and then fry the meat lightly coated in seasoned flour. Mix the curry powder with 1 tsp cumin and ½ cup stock or water and 1 tsp lemon juice. Add to the meat and cook the spices, mixing well. Add half the stock and cook for about 1½ hours over a low heat. Allow to cool and skim off the fat. Add the remaining vegetables and stock, then cook for 30 minutes.

INGREDIENTS

Serves 6

2 tbsp butter
1 large onion, very finely chopped
1 carrot, coarsely grated
½ pound tomatoes
1 small green bell pepper
2 celery stalks, sliced
1 apple, coarsely grated

1 tsp curry powder
2 cloves
1 tbsp chopped parsley
1 tsp coriander
2 tbsp tomato paste
4½ cups chicken stock

1 tbsp cornstarch

⅔ cup milk

1 cup diced cooked chicken

2 tbsp rice, cooked

Game Broth

INGREDIENTS

Serves 6

2 oz pork belly or bacon

¼ cup butter or 2 tbsp
olive oil

1 onion, sliced
2 celery stalks, chopped
selection of broccoli,
snap beans, carrot slices,
mushrooms and diced
turnip

½ cup flour

½ tsp Italian seasoning

⅔ cup sherry or port wine

4 cups game stock
(page 7)

1 tsp lemon juice

2 oz cooked pheasant or
venison, chopped

1   Remove the skin from the meat and cut the flesh into dice.

2   Heat the pork fat with the diced meat until the fat runs out. Add the butter or oil.

3   Add the onion, celery and other vegetables and allow to coat with the fat, turning from time to time. Remove from the pan with a slotted spoon; discard the pork skin. Add the flour and stir until it turns golden brown. Add the sherry or port wine and stock, stirring vigorously.

4   Return all the vegetables to the pan, add the Italian seasoning and simmer for 20 minutes.

5   Season to taste and add the lemon juice for piquancy.

6   Add the meat and reheat.

Corn Chowder

1 Cut the bacon slices
into small pieces. Heat the oil
in a large saucepan, add the bacon and
cook gently. Then turn up the heat and allow to crisp. Add the
onion, turn down the heat and cook for 2 minutes.

2 Add the potato, stir around, then add half the corn kernels
with the chicken stock and seasoning if needed. Bring to a boil
and simmer for 30 minutes. Allow to cool slightly, then purée in a
blender, food processor or food mill.

3 Return to the saucepan and stir in the milk and the remaining corn. Heat through gently. Add the hot-pepper sauce and taste
for seasoning.

VARIATION
This soup can also be served without
being blended. For this method
add all the corn kernels in Step 2,
and gradually stir in the milk at
the end of the cooking time.

INGREDIENTS

Serves 4

4 slices bacon

1 tbsp oil

1 medium onion, chopped

1 potato, cubed

2 cups whole-corn kernels
or frozen whole-corn corn
mixed with bell peppers

2½ cups chicken stock

salt and pepper

1¼ cups milk

¼ tsp hot-pepper sauce

1 tbsp chopped parsley

Index